D1489100

73

Bouquet of Red Flags

ℭჳ

by Taylor Mali

Write Bloody Publishing
America's Independent Press

Austin, TX

WRITEBLOODY.COM

Bouquet of Red Flags

© 2014 Write Bloody Publishing
No part of this book may be used or performed without written consent from the author, except for critical articles or reviews.

Write Bloody
First Edition
ISBN: 9781938912511

Cover art by Ashley Siebels
Proofread by Helen Novielli
Edited by Alex Kryger and Derrick C. Brown
Interior layout by Ashley Siebels
Author photo by Peter Dressel

Type set in Bergamo from www.theleagueofmoveabletype.com

Printed in Tennessee, USA

Write Bloody Publishing
Austin, TX
Support Independent Presses
writebloody.com

To contact the author, send an email to writebloody@gmail.com

MADE IN THE USA

For Jack McCarthy

BOUQUET OF RED FLAGS

OVERWATERING THE GARDEN

There was no problem
in the garden of our marriage
I could not fix with more water.

Always here. Drink in, my love.
I have more to give. Take me
into your roots. Let me drown you.

BOUQUET OF RED FLAGS

OVERWATERING THE GARDEN IX

NOR SHOOTING STARS

LOVE WITHOUT LIMIT, QUESTION, OR WARNING 1
THE LUCK I CRAVE 2
THE NAKED GARDENER.. 3
FRANK McCOURT JOINS BILLY COLLINS
ON THE PATIO AT SUNSET 5
THE TASTE OF SOME WORDS... 6
WHERE I THINK OF YOU 7
EVERY PATH TO GOD IS ALWAYS THE ONLY ONE 8
STALKING THE AIR 9
TRAVELING PRAYER (POSSIBLY UNANSWERED) 10
THE DARLING DAY 11
BOUQUET OF RED FLAGS... 12
SHUT UP AND YOU KNOW I LOVE YOU 13
ON GETTING A VASECTOMY AND HAVING NO CHILDREN 14
THIS IS HOW THEY COME TOGETHER BEST 15
WHEN I HAVE LEFT YOU LONG ENOUGH 16
MAN CAN NEVER KNOW THE RAIN 17
SEEN FROM A LONG WAY OFF 18
AND THEN WE SWITCHED 19

CHAPEL OF RATS

MAGNIFIES AN OBJECT TEN TIMES.. 23
BROKEN THINGS.. 24
CHOCOLATE FOR CALISTO 25
JULY 4, 1990 26
DARK STATION... 27
BASED ON WHAT YOU THINK THE FUTURE HOLDS 28
THE TROUBLED MUDDLE OF THE MIDFIELD 29
WINTER AFTER WINTER..31
DEATH'S FAVORITE... 32

SIMPLE BROKEN WONDER

Nor Shooting Stars

LOVE WITHOUT LIMIT, QUESTION, OR WARNING

Most nights we kiss and then she curls away
eyes already closed. There is no speaking.
But sometime just before the break of day
she turns in sleep to me, her body seeking

mine—or so at least I let myself believe.
Add to the glorious and storied list
of all the daily ills sleep can relieve:
the strain that of a heart can make a fist.

Love without limit, question, or warning.
Sleep and darkness have a way with pain.
I live for moments like the one this morning,
when after weeks of drought, we woke to rain.

THE LUCK I CRAVE

Pennies and four-leaf clovers hardly interest me,
nor shooting stars, nor how you kiss your hand
and touch the dash when driving through a yellow light.

It's the smaller opportunities for luck I crave,
the perfect circles ladybugs have eaten out of leaves,
a family of bats nesting in your house's eaves,

a hummingbird come to find the nectar of your brilliant
crimson scarf. Wishes less well known, like wedding rain,
passing under a moving train, or your initials in a spider's web.

I love the strings and obligations good luck drags behind it
like dented, tin can marriage bells. Driving over railroad tracks
is good luck only if you lift your feet. New moons, blackbirds,

spotted horses, and wagons stacked full of hay: All of these say,
*Go ahead and wish for what you want, but know then
your wish will never come true if you ever look back again.*

THE NAKED GARDENER

You're tired. But there is breakfast to make,
    emails to answer, and poems to write.
You have to submit your manuscript, which means
    making sure the page numbers are right.

So you work out, and stretch, and cool down,
    and head for the sauna when you get the chance:
Strip naked, carry the hamper to the laundry,
    but then remember you have to water the plants.

So nude, you gather your watering can,
    and visit each fern and the bonsai tree,
decide that a cactus cannot be saved:
    And this is how you appear to me.

Naked as Eve in the garden, flushed,
    sweaty hair, a beautiful mess,
a half-dead struggling plant in your hands
    your only natural dress.

You ask me to throw out the cactus,
    say please, and give me a kiss.
But the truth is I would do *anything you want*
    if you asked me naked, like this.

Repave the driveway, learn to speak Latin,
    it doesn't matter the scope of the task.
There's nothing to it. I'm happy to do it:
    Just take off your clothes and ask.

You twirl to continue your rounds,
    leaving me love-struck and smiling wide
until I notice the next plants needing water
    are the ones in the garden . . . outside.

But off you go to tend to your beauties
    watering them one by one.
Radiant woman now only clad
    in the glorious rays of the sun.

I have always considered it fortunate
    that we live on a hill in the middle of the woods,
'cause if the mailman were to come right now
    he'd die from one glimpse of your goods.

O Naked Gardener, carry on
    there is no one but me who can see.
And I hope one day you *feel* as beautiful
    as you *look* every day to me.

FRANK McCOURT JOINS BILLY COLLINS ON THE PATIO AT SUNSET

The two of them, the one with whiskey,
a chilled white wine for the other, watch
as the sun dips into Long Island Sound.

It's a beautiful sunset, says Frank in his brogue,
to which Billy replies, *Back off, McCourt!*
The sunset is my territory. And the sunrise.

You stick to your miserable Irish childhood
and leave us poets the sun and the moon,
which rises even now I call its name.

THE TASTE OF SOME WORDS

That word you said you liked to hear me say?
I will whisper it in your ear all day.
You sleep tight and all night I will lie beside you
slipping it between each dream.

Actions may speak louder than words,
but some come on like shivers, don't come
out but overcome your mouth,
make your lips start speaking in tongues

hips buck and squeeze like *pretty, pretty,*
pretty, pretty please! It's a go down on your knees
kind of thing, like ah (!) bright wings.
Your mouth is open, and your eyes are closed,

your head falls back, and you sing.

WHERE I THINK OF YOU

The American School of London, where once I taught
a rainbow of eighth graders poetry for a week straight,
two times a day, and was so filled with jetlagged happiness,
even though I knew that you and I would never last,
sits in a part of town called St. John's Wood,
two short blocks from Abbey Road,
the street made famous when The Beatles crossed it.

This is where I think of you.

You, whose only reason for never getting a passport before was,
Why should I get a passport if I'll never be able to go anywhere?
A logic I half regret calling *white trash wisdom at its best,*
but which made me suspect you lacked not just imagination,
but a decent dreaming streak.

You received your passport in the mail
on the same day you received your first credit card
and told me it was proof you loved me that you weren't gone.
And so you came to visit me in London.

More than any single tear or desperate caress,
clutching need, or prayer, what I miss now
about you most—what I remember—is your face
when first you saw Abbey Road. That sign. That street.
That corner, and the white stripes of the crosswalk.
How you stopped, and stared, and could not move
like it was a shrine you did not know you sought,
or you, a marble statue in the middle of an empty room
suddenly bursting into bloom.

EVERY PATH TO GOD IS ALWAYS THE ONLY ONE

Bring me to the place where all the things
I know as true are true together at the same time.

Where the world and the people in it are dying,
and everything is also perfect just as it is.

Where the body does not matter, the physical,
the fuck, and is also *all* that matters: heartbeat,
cock, and cunt, and the breath inside the breath.

I want what or whom you choose in this life
to love not to be everything, but to be
at the same time the only thing:
You I choose, and only you.

STALKING THE AIR

Our cat crouches before the fridge and does not budge
except to scratch the floor, as if to ask for more
of the warm air that gently blows from under there,
the price and consequence of making ice
and keeping cold this old house's daily food.

But something in the way he might at any moment pounce
upon the warm and humming air that fills this house
makes me wonder if under there we might have mice
or at least a mouse. And part of me wishes that we do.
In my heart I want to give him that: some tiny thrill

with four feet and a tail to bat about all night
and finally kill come morning, lick bloodless
and leave like some precious gift or warning
outside the front door on the welcome mat.
What greater gift than a mouse to a cat?

TRAVELING PRAYER
(POSSIBLY UNANSWERED)

Sometime early this morning, after I kissed
my sleeping wife goodbye, but before pulling shut
the front door behind me with the quietest click
I could muster, I offered up a silent prayer
that the two strangers sitting in my row
on this transcontinental flight be beautiful,
intelligent, happily married, skinny women;

intelligent so I might learn something new;
and beautiful so I have something nice to look at
while I do—is that so bad to want? I'm a poet,
and it's what we do: we want and we want;
skinny goes without saying, whether male or female,
so they don't ooze or blubber over into my seat
like a beach ball of tepid wet sand; and lastly,
committed and desperately in love so we might
swap stories about coming to know ourselves
looking long into the face of God;

                              but you—you two guys—
whom I have already secretly nicknamed
inside my head Big Mac and The Michelin Man,
you guys are so obviously not what I asked for,
what with your *Golf Digest* and your *Guns & Ammo*,
your ridiculous haircuts, beluga bodies,
and sweaty pinky rings, that I can hardly decide
if today will be the day I finally become an atheist
or whether I believe now more than ever,
as surely and devoutly as any man or woman can,
that the surest way to make God laugh
is just to make a plan.

THE DARLING DAY

Thank God It's Friday is a better name
for a restaurant than *Thank God It's Saturday*
because by then you should already be drunk
or at least nursing a hangover, which is nothing
to thank God for, especially with the weekend
almost over already.

And just to be clear, no one ever named
their place of business *Thank God It's Monday,*
and for good reason.

But once my brother, fond of making
grand pronouncements, declared that
No one ever thinks of Thursday.
This was the same brother whose favorite color
was orange *because he felt sorry for it,*
the one who believed the letter Q
was the envy of the alphabet.

No one ever thinks of Thursday, he said.

Even then, I knew he was dead wrong.
Because everyone thinks of Thursday!
They rarely admit it, but it's the darling day,
the day love letters wait for to be delivered,
and the real beginning of the weekend.

If truth must be told, it's Tuesday no one ever thinks of.

BOUQUET OF RED FLAGS

When first you could not give me yours, mine
did not break because I thought you were a blessing,
blessings being sacred things over which one does not cry.

Later we met and kept meeting, on the streets of New York City,
I now the one with nowhere to put you, the one with the wife
who wasn't you. Or well. I tried to hide what still I carried for you.

Which is to say, you know where I have been, every who
my heart has loved and lost, everything I have given up
in the name of going on. All of what is left of me is yours.

SHUT UP AND YOU KNOW I LOVE YOU, OR, TEACHING "ORIGINS," BY JEFFREY McDANIEL

They're from kitchen cabinets, behind the poison
and insecticides. They're from locked bedroom doors.
They're from dolls and Hunger Games, rock, paper, scissors,
three lives, and you're dead. You're out. You are not my friend.
No. Not it. That seat is taken.

They're from shut up and you know I love you.

They're from get out of my room.
They're from stupid.
They're from fat, ugly, and I hate you.

Shut up and you know I love you.

They're from you're not a part of the real family.
You're adopted. Why do you keep hitting yourself?
Why do you keep hitting yourself?
Look what you made me do.
Mom and Dad said you were a mistake.
They're from please don't tell. This can be our secret.

Two hours of piano every night before dinner.
Do you want the stick? Do I need to get the belt?
Don't make me tell you again. You brought this on yourself.

They're from tears of laughter, and tears,
and I never wanted any of this to happen.
I am so sorry. I promise I'll never do it again.
They're from you know I love you.

This is going to hurt me more than it hurts you.

ON GETTING A VASECTOMY
AND HAVING NO CHILDREN

No second thoughts? asks the nurse
as we walk to the sterile room
where I will be made so as well.
I tell her that my feet are cold,
but that I don't have cold feet.
She laughs because it is cold and true.
But no, I tell her, I am far beyond
second thoughts, which is also true.
Me and you, we have talked about this—
about children—many, many nights,
I who always thought I would marry someone
who wanted them more than I did,
but who married you instead,
and you, who always thought you would as well.
And here we are now, me and this nurse,
walking down the hallway laughing
about cold feet and second thoughts,
last chances, and god damn
her final question, asked
as an afterthought to tuck
the matter into bed:

How many children do you already have?

THIS IS HOW THEY COME TOGETHER BEST

This is how they come together best
when they have been apart for quite a while:
slowly, over several days. It's not a test
of solitude or trial separation. Simply,
they have learned that she should not be home
when at last he does return from having been away.
She needs to spend more time alone—a day
or two—to half prepare and half recover
before her fully life-sized lover ends up coming home.

And truthfully, it must be said that his heart
oozes greedy need and messy glee so he, too,
needs to decompress, spend two nights
alone in bed (yes, uncaressed, but more)
undressed of desperate need. He comes
and sleeps, comes and sleeps, which keeps
his appetites at bay, and all that stuff
that might have seeped or spilled or bled
into her heart—or on the bed—
is kept out of sight, or is rather swept away
as rain can clean the dirty streets at night.

So when they finally meet, love has a chance
to greet the greatest parts of one another,
each lover's heart blossoms in the presence
of the other. Call it romance: the lovely missing
finally over, he kissing her with all his love
until she whispers kisses by themselves
are not enough. Yes, you can guess the rest.
But this is how they come together best.

WHEN I HAVE LEFT YOU LONG ENOUGH

When I have left you long enough
for you to finally want me back,
even maybe miss me some—
a longer length of time for you
than ever it is for me, you needing
as you do at least an hour (if not two)
by yourself, completely alone,
for every one you spend
with someone else (including me);
when I have been away this long
on one of my many trips, I love
the taste of needing in your lips.

MAN CAN NEVER KNOW THE RAIN

Man can never know the rain
even if he swears
he can understand the thunder.

That is not the same as knowing water,
where it comes from, where it runs,
or what it takes with it when it goes,

when one stream flows into another,
then a river, a sea and the ocean,
which never even needs to whisper

Let yourself come into me.

Men will never know the rain
or how to make it come when it is called—
it is only ever chance when clouds appear

to answer to the dancers and the dance.
A man can only ride out the rain,
or cast his moon-face to the sky,

let himself be washed in it. Close his eyes
and pray, *Please come wash over me*
without washing me away.

SEEN FROM A LONG WAY OFF

Those who have waited at the lake's edge,
a summer afternoon of swimming cut short
by the darkening clouds, and watched the rain
advance in a line across the surface of the water,
seen how the spattering reveals the place
that once was still and now is not,

know how it feels to be overcome
by what you cannot change—sorrow,
but also joy—how you sometimes see them
from a distance coming, and know they will soak you
through and through, yet never be ready
for what it feels like when they do.

AND THEN WE SWITCHED

You quoted someone wise,
and said love was the process
of growing closer and closer apart.

And just because I'm like that,
I disagreed, saying it was more like
growing farther and farther together.

But you smiled on the outside,
and I smiled on the inside.
And then we switched.

Chapel of Rats

MAGNIFIES AN OBJECT TEN TIMES

       is what it clearly said
on the handle of the Magnifying Glass
my father received on his fifth birthday.
He took it as a warning; the birthday gift
would only work its magic ten times
and no more, becoming, after that,
just a small round window with no miracle,
toy giant's monocle, a circle of simple glass.

And so he went about his days with curious thrift,
weighing how much he needed to see any part
of the world up close, observing as best he could
with his own eyes first, thinking, *Do I need to see
that dead bug big? That dandelion, that blade
of grass, that wriggling moth in the spider's web?
I can imagine most of nature's gifts and crimes.
Best not to waste one of my ten precious times.*

He lost count of how many miracles he had left,
and for weeks after half expected the magic of the glass
to simply stop. And I have asked him to tell me
of the thrilling moment he realized, or was told,
"ten times" in this context simply meant *tenfold*
and not ten *instances,* but he cannot remember.
Likewise the joy that must have come with such
an infinite epiphany. But what he does recall
and says most he misses still is the way the magic
made him see the world the rest of the time,
not through the glass, but all the time
he thought that magic would not last.

BROKEN THINGS

If I'm attracted to a woman
chances are she's a dancer
and moves with a studied grace,
owns a dog, struggles
with some sort of eating disorder,
is a smoker, or has been raped
at least once in her life.

I've spent a lifetime telling myself
this does not make me ugly
but a lover of beautiful broken things
be they a little dangerous
or just lonely.

Needless to say, any combination
and I am likely to fall in love,
heart under heels.

Which means I fall in love a lot,
such combinations being as likely
as they are tragic, as common
as the bent and broken spokes
on rainy days of all the blown out
umbrellas abandoned in the trash.

Because they cause each other.
The dancer smokes to keep from eating,
or studies and covets her dog's sheer love
of movement, lies with him at night
and whispers *I will die before
I let someone hurt you again.*

CHOCOLATE FOR CALISTO

This is a story about the dogs in my family,
but not about how we named them after local bodies of water
or even about how when I was 20 I finally realized
that only WASPs did that, that the rest of the world
named their dogs whatever they wanted.

This is a story about the dogs in my family,
but not about how we cut a pound of cheddar cheese
into little cubes whenever we took Hudson to the vet,
or, as he came to think of it, *The Place Where I Get Cheese!*
Oh, the things you will let a lab coat do
so long as you get cheddar cheese fed to you
from the hands of the one who loves you best.

Neither is this the story about how my father dug graves
for all our dogs at the family farm months before
any of them died just to insure they could be buried
in the frozen ground if they died in the middle winter;
how we joked that they wondered what the hole was for.
I feel like someone just walked on my grave.

We actually buried Winchester on the morning
of my sister's wedding: *Dearly beloved,
what a beautiful sight. Wedding to the left.
Doggie funeral to the right.* But this isn't a story about that.

This is a story about dogs and chocolate, which they love,
though it can kill them. How, when the time came
to put them down, we gathered and shared with each dog
chocolate like a rich dark sacrament. Who doesn't crave
the taste of their poison?

JULY 4, 1990

The day before my father died,
when I still thought I would see him again,
I told him he was going to live

and that in the years to come,
we would have our own reason
to call this Independence Day.

And I think that's why he died the next day,
just to spare me the burden
of being only half right.

DARK STATION

There is a ghost subway station at 18th Street
on the 6 line in Manhattan, but the trains
don't stop there anymore, which is good
because the exits are all sealed, cemented
and built over, disguised to the point where,
walking above, you can't see where they used to be.

My father had me press my face to the glass
of the car as we shrieked toward Union Square,
my hands cupped to the side of my head
like blinders so I could see better because
the lights are never on. The station is easy to miss,
but it is in all respects like any other station

you might find on the 6 line, except
from 1948, the year it was closed.
I'm comforted by its presence, my father said,
even if I never get to use it. In fact,
especially because I never get to use it.
Like it stands ready for me.

My father dead now almost 25 years,
another exit sealed, I find myself looking
for the station every time I pass,
as though I might catch a glimpse of him
reading his paper, or standing on the platform
looking back at me and waving.

BASED ON WHAT YOU THINK THE FUTURE HOLDS

The surest way to make God laugh is to make a plan.

I remember that time before
my mother started wishing
she would die, but after
she knew she would—
as we all did—in at most
a matter of weeks,
and how even then,
she still had plans for her garden.

You never know anything
except that you will die.
So plant snap peas and dragons,
forsythia, tomatoes, and sun flowers.
Who would deny anyone,
even God, laughter,
that human blessing?

Rain your laughter down over all.

THE TROUBLED MUDDLE OF THE MIDFIELD

The afternoon of the evening my mother was to die
I lingered on the sidelines of a soccer game too long
just to watch the Burden twins do what they do best.
Six minutes between the two, offensive sister
and her defensive twin separated by only six minutes,
except for the entire troubled muddle of the midfield,
that huddled gaggle of other girls who ran crookedly
between the two sisters like a sad flock on stilts.

Jane was the goalie, and she repelled every shot
she did not devour, while Jane—The Other Jane,
that was her name, or rather what we called the younger
just to keep them straight (instead of questioning the inane
logic of their names, *How insane must you be to name
both your daughters Jane?)*—she reigned over the field
at center forward, left foot like a laser beam.

The afternoon of the evening my mother was to die
I prepared two weeks of lesson plans for the teachers
who would take my place while I was away.
And I made a wish that the Girls' Varsity Soccer Team
would one day have a more capable midfield instead
of the cacophony of awkwardness, the never knowing
where to go to be of any use to anyone, which explains
the long balls arcing downfield from the massive volley
of Jane to the sparkling feet of The Other Jane, juking
her way through the stupefied topiary of opposing players.

I suspect there are several ways a man can deal with grief,
but the afternoon of the evening my mother was to die
I watched the Burden twins beat their rivals seven-zero,

watched them for longer than I should have, knowing
I had a four-hour drive to the bedside of still another Jane
and the near certain promise of mourning. My mother died
without me. And it has now been years since the missing
of that moment, the lingering in this riddled life she suffered
waiting for me to tell her what I only hope she knew already.
Still now sometimes when I think of her, I see Jane
and The Other Jane and the wonder of the way they moved,
the one never letting anything in, the way the other
made motionless the world. And also the confusion
of everything in between, midfield of the twin Burdens,
the not knowing how to help or where to run.

WINTER AFTER WINTER

A woman in the elevator reminds me of my mother,
and I tell her—*you have the same style*—curious
shoes and layered jackets buttoned smartly,

a baseball cap, silk scarf, *and glasses dark enough*
to keep most men from talking to you in elevators.
I mean this as a compliment. You are, of course,

much younger than she would have been.
She laughs—she took it as such. And now I notice
that her head is shaved, that she is undergoing

chemo, her cheekbones surfacing like stones
heaved through the earth by frost winter after winter.
I wish the cancer were not part of what made her

look so much like my mother.

DEATH'S FAVORITE

Of all the grieving wails that mourners cry
when I have tucked into earth's final bed
such a one who seemed to lately thrive, my favorite's
How can she be dead when yesterday she was so alive?!

As if there must be some mistake.
As if it somehow made more sense
to take to my side only those who had already died.

But search your heart between the beats.
That momentary stillness knows
that death has only ever graced the living.
And if you read these words, dear reader,
you are still one of those.

SELECTIVE THINNING OF MAPLES

It takes at least a year to fell a tree
because every season tells you something else.
Take one last look at summer's canopy,
and how much shade you can afford to lose.

Every season tells you something else—
winter branches half reveal the view,
how much shade you can afford to lose,
and what you wish to see, and why, and when.

Winter branches half reveal the view, and
more than colors change when autumn comes.
What you wish to see, and why, and when.
Any woodsman worth his axe can tell you,

More than colors change when autumn comes.
So take one last look at summer's canopy.
Any woodsman worth his axe can tell you:
It takes at least a year to fell a tree.

AN AFTERNOON SPENT HANGING ART ON THE WALLS OF OUR NEW APARTMENT

These are the things we find beautiful.
And tonight we hang them on the walls.
There is still a lot to be unpacked, but
we need to have our pictures in place

so tonight we hang them on the walls.
Family photos, flowers, paintings:
we need to have our pictures in place.
A little to the right. Left. The other left.

Family photos, flowers, paintings:
I love looking at you looking at art.
A little to the right. Left. The other left.
Higher. Lower. There that's perfect.

I love looking at you looking at art.
Come let me kiss you all over, love.
Higher. Lower. There that's perfect.
This is what we need to do now.

Come let me kiss you all over, love.
There is still a lot to be unpacked, but
this is what we need to do now, and
these are the things we find beautiful.

AFTER A WEEK ALONE,
NOW WITH ONLY ONE CAT

Your husband is finally home again.
Notice the dirty laundry on the floor.
Say hello to a different kind of solitude.
Chocolate is left like a kiss trail to treasure,

but notice the dirty laundry on the floor
from the bed to the bathroom and everywhere else.
Chocolate left like a kiss trail to treasure.
His body follows you, wanting to be touched

from the bed to the bathroom and everywhere else.
As if you could forget what it's like to live with someone
with his body following you, wanting to be touched.
You don't have to take out the trash. That's something.

You forget what it's like to live with someone,
to have a physical body in addition to a soul.
You don't have to take out the trash. That's something.
And you can still feel the warm place where the cat slept,

a physical body in addition to a soul.
Say hello to a different kind of solitude.
You can still feel the warm place where the cat slept.
Your husband is finally home again.

WHAT THE WHISPERING MEANS

I am shooting rats in a barn with my nephew,
standing in the dead December dark of early night,
his breath beside me and the louder breathing
of goats, dark flashlight in his hand, finger poised
over the button, in mine, a single-shot target pistol,
cocked, pocketful of bullets, one gripped tight
between my teeth. *Shooting rats in a barn,*
you only get one chance, he says. *Two shots, maybe,*
if you're fast. There's a rustle in the hay, and I have fired
already, almost without aim, the weaving tail through the hay,
a miss. And though I know there will be no second shot,
I reload with a bullet from my pocket, forgetting the one
now warm in my mouth. Shooting rats in a barn
is apparently harder than fish in a barrel.
Or fish in a barn, for that matter.
They know what the whispering means.

We wait and listen even though we both know we will return
to the house, the family, his mother, my sister, and my wife
who will kiss my cold cheek. We—my wife and I—
are in a hard place, and because it is what I do, I cannot
help but wonder later if our marriage is the rat, alive
in the chapel of rats, or bleeding out under the hay.
If love be the barn, the warmth, or the flashlight.
If her heart is the breath or the dark; and mine,
the pistol or the bang, the second shot never taken,
this bullet in my mouth.

WHEN I SHOULD HAVE KNOWN

Once I triggered you over something I said
about desire and coming home, something flirty
which landed wrong, like knees on ice, a glass
tumbler on a stone terrace, or a kiss that cracks teeth.

Later I sat down and wrote out what I wished you'd said,
what you could have said, all the words I wanted to hear,
and I gave them to you typed on a clean sheet, asked you
to read them back to me out loud, to try out the taste of them

in your mouth, which you did, even smiling in the places
where I had worked to make them sound like you,
something you might say. *Does that make sense?*
But when you finished and looked up, you were crying.

BEFORE WE GET STARTED

I don't remember her name, but I remember
she wore a black leather jacket, which was odd
for a teacher in Mississippi; cool even
by New York City standards, and I told her so,
said she looked like some urban hipster
I might meet at the Bowery Poetry Club.
This made her smile (I noticed then),
and her day (she told me later).

But this is not about the way she looked
but how she sounded when she sang,
which she did—which they asked her to do,
the national anthem—at the start of the meeting.
If we could all rise and place our hands over our hearts,
which I did, it being Mississippi, after all.
And this was apparently what they did here.
With straight faces no less, and not the least trace
of sarcasm, ennui, or even irony. It was patriotic,
of course, but not in the same way protesting
the war or burning the flag can be patriotic,
but patriotic nevertheless.

Listen, all I want to say is that I admired her
and her clear, brave, patriotic, unironic voice.
Even her *And the rocket's red glare,*
the bombs bursting in air, which everyone knows
is the hardest part, rang out strong
and floated over our heads in the Mississippi air
like a flag in the dawn's early light.

THE NEED FOR THE NEW LOVE

"the need
for the new love is faithfulness to the old."
—Galway Kinnell

Something in the way she left me
this time made it easier to let her go.
Perhaps it was in the way she let me know
how hard it is for me to be alone
when she is gone, how I mope like the dog,
drink too much, and eat too much
(also like the dog), and stay up too late
then sleep too long. Like the dog.

But this time, I fed
the cats when they needed
feeding and even worked out
a few times, every single
pull-up and push-up
a tug of war with my body.

And yet when she returns I tell her
I do not like to be alone the way
she likes to be alone, that three weeks
is almost too hard for me.
I had a glimpse of what my life
would be if I were alone again,
if I—Dear Lord, I said, let me not
lose another wife—I would, I think,
what I want to say: I do not know
what I would do then. "I do," she said,
"You would marry again."

Simple Broken Wonder

THE SPELL, UNUSED

We are no longer married, but yesterday
   I recited a love poem I wrote
for you when we still were to an audience

because, I said, *I still like the poem.*
   And everyone laughed because
it sounded as if I meant I didn't still like you.

Which got me started on how not everything
   is meant to last forever,
how some people see it before others, and why

what makes a good poem, be it a certain vein,
   or grain of sand inside a pearl,
doesn't always make a good marriage.

I told a roomful of strangers that every love poem
   I ever wrote for you tried
to tell me this truth: that you would one day leave.

I asked the audience to see if they could hear
   that truth in this poem, too.
It's the one about how your body has a power

over me, and how I could never say no to you
   when you went without clothes.
After the reading, a woman told me what went wrong

with us. *You gave your wife a secret spell,* she said.
   A power over you she never used.

LOVE AS A FORM OF DIVING

It could be words do not exist
to make you fall deeper
in love with me.

Or else they do, but I don't know them.

Or I do, the words,
but not the order,
the exact proportions of each one,
or the secret of how they fit together,
thinking they do as bodies do, like ours.

But maybe nothing
is for you an act of falling,
a hunger, or a hunkering;
like love, which is for me
a kind of burrowing,
a sinking into ripening,
and yet for you is more like flying—
taut wings of the hawks overhead,
circling, now closer, now more apart,
haunting some thermal of the heart.

THERE IS ALWAYS MORE—

you cannot know—
more love, more motion,
another level of devotion,
or a different door
with a different kind of handle
on the other side.
There is the dark,
and here, a candle.
Sit still and silent, practice;
straighten the slouch
of the pain-bent back.

There is always more—
you cannot know—
as when in the midst of rain
it starts to rain harder,
with more drench
and wail, be it the wind,
the force of the gale,
or something else
walled inside you
that called it forth—
what tear, what tide,
what drenched
and unexpected holy joy:
you cannot know—
but something in you
called it forth and wants it so.

THE JUMPERS

No one can jump into the arms of God.
You have to fall.

—Tom Junod, *Esquire*

When fire sealed the fate of all above that ragged mouth—
and many more below—there came a time when some of those
who knew their death would be that day chose to jump
instead of stay and burn. The Jumpers, they were called.

Although, as I would later learn, it was a turn of phrase
the coroner did not prefer to use in any way when he referred
to that Tuesday in September's dead. *No one jumped that day,*
he said. The photos, of course, tell a different side.

And some Catholic families of those who died have always
denied any image of a falling body was a husband, sister, or a son;
they say they were blown out, or forced out, or simply fell,
because anyone who died by jumping would forever burn in hell.

That is a burning I cannot speak to. And little comfort may come
from what I now say, but I saw them all that day from my roof
two miles away. All of them—the couple who held hands,
the man who soared with arms outstretched like useless wings,

alone, the flailing legs, the fluttering of every mortal stone—
and I found in their falling a beauty, some particle of grace,
a shard of stained salvation glass, and although I cannot say
exactly why, I will cling to their mortal flight until I, too, die.

STAR OF THIS MORNING'S DREAM

What characterizes the human race more:
cruelty, or the capacity to feel shame for it?
          —*from Shantaram, by Gregory David Roberts*

I woke this morning dreaming of Star
and the afternoon we broke up; how we sat
together on the sofa while I itemized to her face
the ways she had failed me, fallen short—
who it was I had hoped she might become
in the presence of my love and who it was instead
I had in hers; of how, then, when I least expected it,
she hauled off and kissed me hard on the lips,
and pulled away apologizing. She's sorry, she said.
She didn't mean to do that, she said. It's just
that she's so wet. *And I couldn't help myself.*

And I was going to write this morning for an hour
about the folly of the human heart:
Why it is we want the one who is already gone,
who says we're not good enough. Except
what I did then was slip my hand between her legs
to see if she was telling the truth,
and *that* seems the more intricate act
of human cruelty in need of exploration with my pen.

In the morning's memory I do awful things
I never did that afternoon like ask if she wants
what her heart cannot have. In memory I make her
into a slut who I took one last time so madly
it was exactly what she wanted.

I tell myself that it was breakup sex, which is always awesome
for one of you at least, the one who will leave anyway, the body
of the other saying in every buck and thrust and bitter grind
Stay or you will never feel this again. But the truth is
I was mean then and meaner still in my memory this morning.
Why do I come to this? Why would I want to?
I have seen such ugliness inside myself and wished
I did not recognize any of it.

THE BRICK HOUSE PUB IN HOUSATONIC

We sit at the mill town bar and stare
into our drinks with faces red and vacant
as the brick mills that employed our fathers
and grandfathers, eyes broken like the panes
we busted with rocks when we were young.

And when we hear the train rumble its weight
through town, so close the screeching metal
calls to us to lay our tattooed necks on the rails,
we resist, step outside only to watch it pass.

Smoking, we look up to the passing train
like for redemption or forgiveness, or more
in simple broken wonder, like it is our moon.

MY DEEPEST CONDIMENTS

I send you my deepest condiments
was in no way what my old friend
meant to say or write or send
the night she penned a note to me
one week after my father died.

Not *condolences*, or *sentiments*,
she sent me her deepest condiments
instead, as if the dead have need
of relish, mustard, and ketchup
on the other side.

O, the word made me laugh
so hard out loud it hurt!
So wonderfully absurd,
and such a sweet relief
at a time when it seemed

only grief was allowed in
after my father's death,
sweet and simple laughter,
which is nothing more than
breath from so far deep inside

it often brings up with it tears.
And so I laughed and laughed
until my sides were sore.
And later still, I even cried
a little more.

WITH OR WITHOUT LAUGHTER

Laura of the long legs used to make me laugh
while we made love because she said my laughter
turned her on, opened and melted her in places
nothing else could fit inside of or even reach.
But also because we had discovered the simple act
of laughing made me last longer in bed—a bait
and switch of sweet releases. It worked, for what
is laughter but a way to make you breathe more deeply,
as prayer is just a way to make you ask for what you want
from *goddamn*, the sex was wonderful!

Even though it sounded like a secret back room
at a comedy strip club. You've heard of *talking dirty?*
She talked *funny*, whispered first into my ear silly things
like *cumquat, marshmallow, didgeridoo*. And,
You know, a funny thing happened on the way to my vagina.

And I would laugh full bodied and somehow keep on going
while she ground herself against my ha-ha-ha.

But soon I was laughing at her attempts to be funny
in the midst of her arousal, the breathless comic genius
gasping out gems like, "What's the difference between Jesus
and . . . O God!" Curious *kōans* in which you couldn't tell
if the humor had been hijacked by the sex, or if the point—
like love—was that there was no answer.

Maybe I have had better sex since Laura, with or without
laughter, but what sometimes I have missed was the way
we fit together, how it grew more perfect over time,
like a bed that creaks less the more it rocks, or an itch
that blossoms under a better scratch.

THE LEAST INVESTMENT

I have drifted from one woman to another
my whole life. But never far, and always between
two kinds I called Good Girls and Bad Girls
because I didn't know any better.

There were bad girls who never drank, who drove
the speed limit to volunteer in soup kitchens,
and good girls with filthy mouths who only came
with their hair pulled gently back. That wasn't it.

The good girls all loved me a little more
than I loved them, and the bad girls were the opposite.
The more they *didn't* love me back, the worse they were.
Turns out after everything, that's all it was.

THINGS TO WHICH I HAVE COMPARED OUR MARRIAGE

A wave, a sunset, a solar eclipse, a star, a shooting star, a black hole, an undiscovered planet, an unlit candle, the last match, a bird's nest with two blue eggs (like the one we had to move off the flood lamp, knowing the chicks would never hatch); as a fish you can never catch, a nudibranch, shark, a piece of coral, the breath, the dark, a walk in the woods, the snow, the morning, a beach, as a fire in the fireplace that lights from a spark or embers, as a three-legged dog, two cats, one dead mouse licked clean like a loving gift, granite, quartz, sandstone, fool's gold, a pebble on our driveway, black ice, rain, the ocean, thirteen million undulating jellyfish (and how you emerged from the lake with tears in your eyes for the love of God); as a sprint, the marathon, the broad jump, the hurdles, a nap, a dream, a bath, a hundred-thousand -dollar bill, the Sacagawea dollar coin, a first edition, the last will and testament, the cool side of the pillow, a pasta machine, a queen size bed, a single bed, sleeping alone in a king size bed in a hotel room, a good night's rest on a hardwood floor; as a vacation, a second home, a luxury, an extravagance, a lightning bolt, a bat, a chant, a game, a tear, glove, tree, stone, nail, needle, silver bullet, a drug, an antibacterial ointment, a balm, a time bomb, a heart attack, a computer, database, hard drive, a trust fund, a glimpse, an epiphany, a mirror, a view of the river, a window, a door, a gateless gate, a gong, a call to prayer; as electricity, a dead light bulb, a dry well, a flat tire, a spare tire, a pair of favorite pants that no longer fit and never will, neatly hanging in the closet; aloha.

DIVORCE

I could not meet you
in every joyous way
you needed to be met
to live, and so it was
I wanted more,
and needed more,
and gave you too much more,
had even more to give.

GIVE IT AWAY OR PUT IT AWAY OR THROW IT AWAY

At the end of the marriage,
whatever stuff is left—
like crutches or rustic tools
you rarely used, tight shoes,
dusty books, or even love—
whatever lies piled on the floor
you have to find a way to store
after the divorce. Unless
of course *before* that day
you took the time to give away

or sell (at a tag sale or on eBay)
all that did not break apart
in the course of breaking up
your home and heart,
some of it, no doubt, cracked
from the start, or else
abandoned in the name
of moving on and living;
everything must be given away,
or in some other way forgiven.

What's left must be stored somewhere,
be it in the flood-cursed basement
of a friend, or worse, the rented
metal room where love, like wine,
goes to improve but never does.
Or, at least, the body, let loose
in memory's uncharted attic,
or left undressed in some empty
chamber, say, the 5 by 10 container
in the middle in your chest.

HOW TO SPELL L–O–V–E

Before we were married—after I had already begun to suspect I could not meet you in every sacred way you needed to be met, but long before this suspicion of insufficiency had grown inside you into the tumorous need to dump me, a devastation I once described accidentally to a friend as *having the plug pulled out from under me*—you and I sat in the sun-drenched lobby of a bank and opened a checking account together.

When the time came for each of us to pick our own secret PINs, personal identification numbers, the bank manager slid the key-pad over to you, but you hesitated, your fingers hovering over the keypad. You told the manager, as if in warning, *I have a number that I often use, but some systems won't accept it.* He advised you not to use 0-0-0-0 or 1-2-3-4, but you said it was nothing like that, so he told you to go ahead and try the number and see what happened. You did.

And almost immediately it was obvious something wasn't quite right. There was a beep, or a buzz, or maybe the screen flashed, but sure enough, the computer wouldn't take your PIN.

In the end you had to use a different number, presumably more "normal." The manager said he'd never seen that before, but I sat beside you the whole time, green with curiosity. What number could you have possibly chosen that would have brought the bank to its knees?! *Please, Miss, any number except that number!* There are only 10,000 possibilities, and there's one that doesn't work?! Why didn't I know this number?!

I asked you what it was, but you smiled and wouldn't tell me. And why should you? Presumably the PIN still worked with other things, other accounts, secret accounts of a higher order capable of processing the mystical power of your special number. So in my mind, the number got added to the list of ways I feared I was not good enough for you, one of the things a better man would have already known. If I could whisper that number in your ear, would I gain fuller access to your heart? Could I have withdrawn from you unlimited amounts of love and longing?

Flash forward to yesterday when a friend told me that 5683 is one of the most common four-digit PINS because it spells LOVE. The number is so common that many systems will refuse to accept it. Was that it? Was that all it was? Was it 5683? Was it LOVE?

SONNET ON MY WEDDING RING AND OTHER THINGS I THINK I'VE LOST

The body forgets at a different pace
than does the mind. Washing my hands,
splashing cold water on my face,
I'm suddenly jolted when memory demands
to know what's happened to my wedding ring,
which is indeed missing from my finger.
I close my eyes and try to bring
to mind the band, stumble, then linger
on this fact I'd not remembered:
it is late October and I'm not married anymore;
I've been divorced since mid-September
and haven't worn the ring for three months. Maybe four.
I don't think I miss the ring—or even you—
but my fingers and my hands? Apparently they do.

DANCE WITH THE ONE WHO BRUNG YOU, OR, MY NIGHT IN A GAY COWBOY BAR IN DALLAS, TEXAS

A redneck working on an MFA,
two gay Texans, a blonde in a miniskirt
and cowboy boots, and a poet from New York City
all walk into a gay cowboy bar in Dallas, Texas.
This is not a joke.

It is the week before Christmas and the dance floor
is filled with cowboys dancing the Texas Two-Step
and holding each other lovely and close, here
where the threat of being beaten to death
has been banished to the long drive home,
or at least the parking lot outside.
This is not a joke.

This is something I was told I had to see
because we don't have anything like it in New York City.
It is the week before Christmas, and there is one old
jolly white-bearded cowboy in his mid-seventies
dressed up to look like just like Santa Claus.
If Santa Claus ever went to a gay cowboy bar in Dallas, Texas.
Or New York City for that matter.

Neither of the gay Texans will dance with Jason,
the redneck, and I know this because I watch him
get shot down twice, both of them laughing
and holding each other's hand a little harder
as if to say, *We will not take part in what, for you,
will no doubt be in time just a funny story.*
This is not a joke.

And of course, to waltz the floor in a gay cowboy bar
with a woman, even if she is blonde, wears a hat
like a rodeo, and rocks red lipstick like a bloody mouth—
especially for all of this—would be disrespectful.
A redneck knows this. So Jason doesn't ask.

And it must be because I am also not gay
that Jason doesn't ask me to dance,
which, under the circumstances,
seems not to be a good enough reason.
So it is I who asks him. And we take each other
in our arms and dance, as best we can,
the only two straight guys in the bar.
Or so it seems to us, which is why we laugh
while we dance, our friends at the table laughing, too,
and wishing that among them someone had a camera.

This was long ago. And I can hear in the memory
of that laughter now other minor strains of fear,
and shame, and privilege—this is not a joke—
but the major tones are merely love and joy.
And that's how I remember the night Jason and I
danced in a gay cowboy bar in Dallas, Texas.

WRITING A DIFFERENT SONG

If the top half of a boulder emerges from the earth
like a giant's skull surfacing the field, bramble covered,
with thistle and scotch broom twisted and sunk
so deep into each other you need to take two passes each
with machete and chainsaw, and each again, just to clear
the way for the other's work;

if the brush roots rip out earth and moss
when they finally come crackling, and reveal
the naked rock to you, the sun, and air;

if both your parents had died of cancer, that pebbly sorrow,
and you were the kind of man to take it out on the land,
to give voice to stones you could then crack with flint rage,
or take offense at branches and break them off as payback
at the trunk; feel free for once to write a different song.

Feel free not to see as cancer this time the lovely stone.
Be grateful simply to have known love. This time,
you can root for the rock.

HAVE AND TO HOLD

I want to be the one who was left
as well as the one who moved on
and found a better love, which seems
to me somehow selfish, greedy,
and therefore human, to hold hard
to the hurt in one hand
but have the other open and empty.
There is a way of nursing a wound
that keeps it new and beautiful,
as ragged as the day it bloomed.
But to heal the body must forget
or at least forgive every injustice
done to it for any reason, especially
those exacted in the name of love.

NIGHTFALL

When I go
I want to go
in the same way
night is said to fall.

Because it is day
that does the falling,
while night
at the other end
of the twilit sky,
to take its place,
rises to the evening.

DEDICATIONS

"The Taste of Some Words" is for Sarah Sears

"Where I Think of You" and "Star of This Morning's Dream" are for Aurora. You helped me during a difficult time in my life, and I treated you unfairly.

"Dance with the One Who Brung You" is for Jason Carney

"The Darling Day" is for my brother Peter Mali

"Chocolate for Calisto" is for Jeanann Verlee

"Before We Get Started" is for Laurie Roberts. As it turns out, you are from Idaho and not Mississippi, but I didn't know that when I mistakenly figured our paths would never cross again.

"Magnifies an Object Ten Times" is for Charles Brainerd. As you know, this poem is actually based on your dad, not mine.

"Based on What You Think the Future Holds" is for my sister Adair Mali

"Selective Thinning of Maples" is for my godmother Barbara Roberts

"What the Whispering Means" is for my nephew Winston Pingeon

"My Deepest Condiments" is for Ursula Sneed

"With or Without Laughter" is for Linnea Pyne. This was your discovery with an old boyfriend who was not me. But I've found it to be true, too.

"Death's Favorite" is for Maggie Estep and Seth Rogovoy

"How to Spell L-O-V-E" is for April Ranger. You are the friend in this poem, and I hope you still will be even now that everyone knows your PIN.

"Broken Things" is for Eric Guerrieri. You noticed this about yourself, mentioned it once out loud to me over Steve Jobs's whiskey, and I stole it and used it in a poem of my own because that's what I do.

And all the divorce poems are for my former wife, Marie-Elizabeth Mali, who flew with me like Icarus until we came to "the end of our triumph."

ACKNOWLEDGEMENTS

Thanks to Rachel who knows that writing these poems was part of my process. To my mom and dad with whom I speak daily despite their deaths over 20 years ago. To the elderly woman who, after one of my readings, told me I was "the Billy Collins of [my] generation—except even worse!" To Jeffery McDaniel for all his metaphors. I couldn't have written this book without the encouragement, love, and prodding of my former second-best friend Cristin O'Keefe Aptowicz. Finally, this book is dedicated to Jack McCarthy, to whom I wrote over two dozen postcards in the last year of his life. Consider this book another one.

And many thanks to the following journals where many of these poems first appeared, sometimes in earlier versions:

Naugatuck River Review: "What the Whispering Means"

Poemeleon: "The Brick House Pub in Housatonic" and "An Afternoon Hanging Art on the Walls of Our New Apartment"

Aerie International: "Traveling Prayer (Possibly Unanswered)"

Barnwood: "The Taste of Some Words"

Cadillac Cicatrix: "And Then We Switched"

Jelly Bucket: "The Luck I Crave"

Man Box: "Star of This Morning's Dream"

Muzzle: "Broken Things"

O & S: "The Darling Day"

Literary Mixtape: "Love as a Form of Diving"

Texas A & M: "Selective Thinning of Maples" and "Nightfall"

The Burden of Light: Poems on Illness & Loss: "Based on What You Think the Future Holds"

Tribeca Review: "Dark Station"

Used Furniture Review: "Benediction for the Morning," "Chocolate for Calisto," "The Naked Gardener"

Whatever Literary Journal: "Every Path to God is Always the Only One"

Rattle: "Magnifies an Object Ten Times"

Kalyna Review: "My Deepest Condiments," "With or Without Laughter," "The Spell, Unused"

STUDY QUESTIONS & DISCUSSION STARTERS

1. Taylor Mali has been teaching poetry workshops all over the world since 2000. If you've had him as a teacher, you've probably heard him say "a poem is the perfect place to celebrate imperfection and exult in the ways you fall short of being the person you want to be." In what poems does Mali do that himself? Pick a few lines from a few poems and talk about how they can be seen as celebrations of the imperfect.

2. Since 2001 Taylor Mali has been sharing his poetry every couple months with the residents of Brown Gardens, a senior living community on the Upper East Side of Manhattan. During a recent visit, he read several poems from this collection that are about forgiveness, letting go, and moving on. "Or so I thought. But after one poem, a regular named Miriam announced that I obviously hadn't taken responsibility for my own part in the failure of my marriage. But that's why I wrote the poems in the first place! Isn't it?" Pick a few poems and discuss the extent to which they are honest explorations of culpability or just artful and eloquent excuses.

3. In the poem "The Spell, Unused," the persona writes "what makes a good poem, be it a certain vein, or grain of sand inside a pearl, doesn't always make a good marriage." Do you think that's true? Is some kind of irritant necessary for the creation of lasting beauty in a poem? Or a relationship? Or anything other than a pearl? Is there a difference between growing "closer and closer apart" and growing "farther and farther together"?

4. In the poem "Magnifies an Object Ten Times," a young boy mistakenly believes his new magnifying glass will only work ten times. Consequently, he cultivates a thrifty kind of observation, rife with wonder, so as not to needlessly waste the glass's magic

power. Could that serve as a kind of poetic manifesto for Taylor Mali's poetry as a whole? In what other poems do you see evidence of a careful observation as though the "magic [will] not last"?

5. A common theory put forth by self-help books and "love gurus" is that the power in any relationship lies with the one who cares the *least*. Find a poem or two that might suggest Mali would agree or disagree.

6. After hearing "The Jumpers" in Louisville, KY, during the AP English Exam grading week in June of 2013, one teacher wrote Mali and asked if she could use the then-unpublished poem on a practice exam at her own school. He sent the poem along with the following note explaining how the poem came about:

> It must have been an interview with Tom Junod on NPR where I first heard the heartbreaking fact that many Catholic families of the restaurant workers who died on September 11th refused to even look at photographs of those who had jumped to their deaths because that would mean—at least in their minds—that their loved ones had committed suicide and earned a one-way ticket to hell. Later I read Junod's article about trying to discover the identity of the person depicted in the iconic photo called The Falling Man. He repeated there the attitude of many Catholics toward those who chose to jump from the burning towers. I think there's even a quotation in the essay where someone looked at the photo and said, "That piece of shit is not my father." I wrote "The Jumpers" with a desire to honor that last flight instead of condemn it.

> I carried the first few lines around for a couple years in my head and jangled them together like change in my pocket. I particularly liked the image of the "ragged mouth" because that's what the hole in the north tower looked like to me, two miles away, on the morning of September 11th, 2001.

I don't know for sure, but I suspect everyone above the points of impact in both towers died that day, either by fire, impact, smoke inhalation, or jumping. And I'd like to think that if I were in that impossible situation, I would have jumped if I'd had the chance.

There's another thing you should know when you read this poem, and that is that my first wife committed suicide by jumping out the window of our apartment building on September 13th, three years later, in 2004. She was depressed, and in her journals she wrote that she felt it was her calling to "heal the anger of the victims of September 11th." Apparently, she felt she could do more good on the other side. She's not in this poem at all, but there's another poem of mine called "Depression, Too, is a Kind of Fire" that is about what it takes to make a human being decide to jump out of a building.

Finally, I'm remarried now, and my wife Rachel recently told me that in Judaism one is compelled to do *everything one can to stay alive.* So from a spiritual perspective, jumping out the window was actually the correct thing to do because staying meant *certain* death. She has heard several rabbis say that it's possible some helicopter could have caught the people who jumped. They didn't *know for sure* they would die if they jumped. But they knew they would if they stayed. So those who jumped did so because they desperately wanted to live. That to me deserved a poem. At the very least.

What do you think? Would you have jumped? Would it have been an act of defeat or defiance? Or is that the wrong question to ask? Seek out "Depression, Too, is a Kind of Fire" and read it in relation to "The Jumpers" and the note above.

photo by Peter Dressel

ABOUT TAYLOR MALI

Since June of 2000 Taylor Mali has been a touring poet and itinerant creative writing teacher. A four-time National Poetry Slam champion, he is the author of two previous collections of poetry, *What Learning Leaves* and *The Last Time As We Are,* and a book of essays, *What Teachers Make: In Praise of the Greatest Job in the World.* He lives in Brooklyn where he helps curate the poetry reading series Page Meets Stage.

IF YOU LOVE TAYLOR MALI, TAYLOR MALI LOVES . . .

The Year of No Mistakes
by Cristin O'Keefe Aptowicz

After the Witch Hunt
by Megan Falley

Drunks & Other Poems of Recovery
by Jack McCarthy

Floating, Brilliant, Gone
by Franny Choi

No Matter the Wreckage
by Sarah Kay

Write Bloody Publishing distributes and promotes great books of fiction, poetry, and art every year. We are an independent press dedicated to quality literature and book design, with an office in Austin, TX.

Our employees are authors and artists, so we call ourselves a family. Our design team comes from all over America: modern painters, photographers, and rock album designers create book covers we're proud to be judged by.

We publish and promote 8 to 12 tour-savvy authors per year. We are grass-roots, D.I.Y., bootstrap believers. Pull up a good book and join the family. Support independent authors, artists, and presses.

Want to know more about Write Bloody books, authors, and events?
Join our mailing list at

www.writebloody.com

WRITE BLOODY BOOKS

After the Witch Hunt — Megan Falley

Aim for the Head, Zombie Anthology — Rob Sturma, Editor

Amulet — Jason Bayani

Any Psalm You Want — Khary Jackson

Birthday Girl with Possum — Brendan Constantine

The Bones Below — Sierra DeMulder

Born in the Year of the Butterfly Knife — Derrick C. Brown

Bouquet of Red Flags —Taylor Mali

Bring Down the Chandeliers — Tara Hardy

Ceremony for the Choking Ghost — Karen Finneyfrock

Clear Out the Static in Your Attic — Rebecca Bridge & Isla McKetta

Courage: Daring Poems for Gutsy Girls — Karen Finneyfrock, Mindy Nettifee & Rachel McKibbens, Editors

Dear Future Boyfriend — Cristin O'Keefe Aptowicz

Dive: The Life and Fight of Reba Tutt — Hannah Safren

Drunks and Other Poems of Recovery — Jack McCarthy

The Elephant Engine High Dive Revival anthology

Everyone I Love Is A Stranger To Someone — Anneleyse Gelman

Everything Is Everything — Cristin O'Keefe Aptowicz

The Feather Room — Anis Mojgani

Floating, Brilliant, Gone — Franny Choi

Gentleman Practice — Buddy Wakefield

Glitter in the Blood: A Guide to Braver Writing — Mindy Nettifee

Good Grief — Stevie Edwards

The Good Things About America — Derrick Brown and Kevin Staniec, Editors

The Heart of a Comet — Pages D. Matam

Hot Teen Slut — Cristin O'Keefe Aptowicz

I Love Science! — Shanny Jean Maney

I Love You is Back — Derrick C. Brown

CPSIA information can be obtained
at www.ICGtesting.com
Printed in the USA
FSOW01n1028270217
31238FS